To:

From

believe

Written and compiled by
Suzanne Schwalb

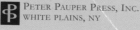

Peter Pauper Press, Inc.
White Plains, NY

Designed by David Cole Wheeler

Copyright © 2009
Peter Pauper Press, Inc.
202 Mamaroneck Avenue
White Plains, NY 10601
ISBN 978-1-59359-848-8
Printed in China
14

Visit us at www.peterpauper.com

believe

"Magic is believing in yourself," said Goethe. "If you can do that, you can make anything happen." Let this little book of wisdom help you work that magic. Take its words to heart as you pursue your dreams. Believe, and live by your beliefs. Persist, and make stepping stones of stumbling blocks. The key to your life is within you right now. Take it, and unlock the door to life's possibilities.

Nothing splendid has ever been achieved except by those who dared believe that something inside of them was superior to circumstance.

BRUCE BARTON

Cherish your visions and
your dreams as they are the
children of your soul;
the blueprints of your
ultimate achievements.

 NAPOLEON HILL

We are all part of creation, all kings, all poets, all musicians; we have only to open up, to discover what is already there.

HENRY MILLER

Our remedies oft in
ourselves do lie,
Which we ascribe
to heaven.

WILLIAM SHAKESPEARE,

ALL'S WELL THAT ENDS WELL

Only in the darkness
can you see the stars.

MARTIN LUTHER KING, JR.

To be yourself in
a world that is constantly
trying to make you
something else is the
greatest accomplishment.

RALPH WALDO EMERSON

If you're going
through hell,
keep going.

WINSTON CHURCHILL

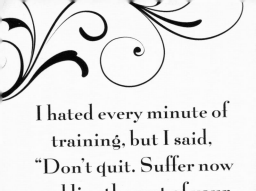

I hated every minute of training, but I said, "Don't quit. Suffer now and live the rest of your life as a champion."

MUHAMMAD ALI

It's kind of fun to
do the impossible.

WALT DISNEY

Be yourself;
everyone else is
already taken.

OSCAR WILDE

You'll never find
a rainbow if you're
looking down.

CHARLIE CHAPLIN

I am not afraid . . .
I was born to do this.

JOAN OF ARC

I know God won't give me
anything I can't handle.
I just wish He didn't
trust me so much.

MOTHER TERESA

If you are going to try, go all the way or don't even start. If you follow it, you will be alive with the gods. It is the only good fight there is.

CHARLES BUKOWSKI

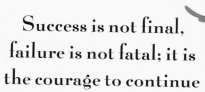

Success is not final,
failure is not fatal; it is
the courage to continue
that counts.

WINSTON CHURCHILL

First they ignore you,
then they ridicule you,
then they fight you,
and then you win.

MAHATMA GANDHI

Fall seven times,
stand up eight.

Follow your bliss
and don't be afraid,
and doors will open
where you didn't know
they were going to be.

JOSEPH CAMPBELL

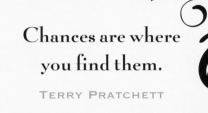

Chances are where
you find them.

TERRY PRATCHETT

Pain is temporary.
Quitting lasts forever.

LANCE ARMSTRONG

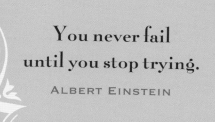

You never fail
until you stop trying.

ALBERT EINSTEIN

Ninety percent of the game
is half mental.

YOGI BERRA

Yesterday is history.
Tomorrow is mystery.
Today is a gift.
That's why we call it
"the present."

ELEANOR ROOSEVELT

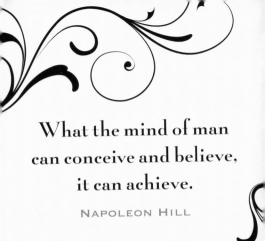

What the mind of man
can conceive and believe,
it can achieve.

NAPOLEON HILL

Dream barriers look very high until someone climbs them. Then they are not barriers anymore.

LASSE VIRÉN

A journey of
a thousand miles
begins with
a single step.

CONFUCIUS

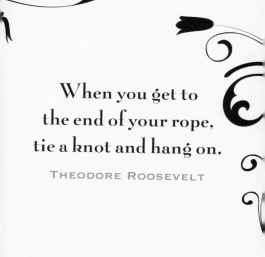

When you get to
the end of your rope,
tie a knot and hang on.

THEODORE ROOSEVELT

Man imposes
his own limitations,
don't set any.

ANTHONY BAILEY

Human beings are
made up of flesh and
blood, and a miracle
fiber called courage.

GEORGE PATTON

All you have to do
is know where you're going.
The answers will come to
you of their own accord.

EARL NIGHTINGALE

The power of one is above all the power to believe in yourself, often beyond any ability you may have previously demonstrated. The mind is the athlete, the body is simply the means it uses.

BRYCE COURTENAY

Some people say I have
attitude—maybe I do.
But I think you have to.
You have to believe in
yourself when no one else
does—that makes you
a winner right there.

VENUS WILLIAMS

Bite off more than you
can chew, then chew it.

ELLA WILLIAMS

It is just as easy to see
yourself successful as it is
to see yourself a failure,
and far more interesting.

AUTHOR UNKNOWN

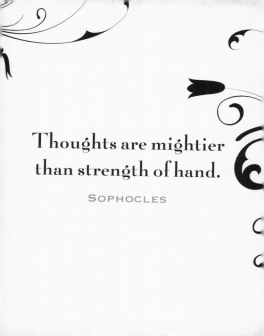

Thoughts are mightier
than strength of hand.

SOPHOCLES

What lies behind us
and what lies before us
are tiny matters compared
to what lies within us.

RALPH WALDO EMERSON

The trick is in what one emphasizes. We either make ourselves miserable, or we make ourselves happy. The amount of work is the same.

CARLOS CASTANEDA

To be champ, you have to
believe in yourself when
nobody else will.

SUGAR RAY ROBINSON

If you hear a voice within you say "you cannot paint," then by all means paint, and that voice will be silenced.

VINCENT VAN GOGH

Plant your own garden
and decorate your own
soul, instead of waiting
for someone to bring
you flowers.

VERONICA A. SHOFFSTALL

Live by what you believe
so fully that your life
blossoms, or else purge the
fear-and-guilt producing
beliefs from your life....
Live your belief, or
let that belief go.

ROGER JOHN

The thing always happens that you really believe in; and the belief in a thing makes it happen.

FRANK LLOYD WRIGHT

Sometimes
I've believed as many
as six impossible things
before breakfast.

LEWIS CARROLL,
THROUGH THE LOOKING GLASS

Twenty years from now
you will be more disappointed
by the things that you didn't
do than by the ones you did do.
So throw off the bowlines.
Sail away from the safe harbor.
Catch the trade winds
in your sails.
Explore. Dream. Discover.

MARK TWAIN

Lend yourself to others,
but give yourself
to yourself.

MICHEL DE MONTAIGNE

The universe is change;
our life is what our
thoughts make it.

MARCUS AURELIUS

It's the repetition
of affirmations that
leads to belief. And
once that belief becomes
a deep conviction, things
begin to happen.

CLAUDE M. BRISTOL

Confidence comes not from always being right but from not fearing to be wrong.

PETER T. MCINTYRE

Self-trust is the first
secret of success.

RALPH WALDO EMERSON

I am the master of my fate;
I am the captain of my soul.

WILLIAM ERNEST HENLEY

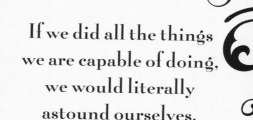

If we did all the things
we are capable of doing,
we would literally
astound ourselves.

THOMAS EDISON

The way to develop
self-confidence is to do
the thing you fear and get a
record of successful
experiences behind you.
Destiny is not a matter
of chance, it is a matter of
choice; it is not a thing to
be waited for, it is a thing
to be achieved.

WILLIAM JENNINGS BRYAN

All that we are
is the result of
what we have thought.

BUDDHA

In truth, one step at a time
is not too difficult. . . .
I know that small attempts,
repeated, will complete
any undertaking.

OG MANDINO

It's time to start living
the life you've imagined.

HENRY JAMES

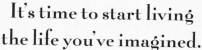

Most people achieved their greatest success one step beyond what looked like their greatest failure.

BRIAN TRACY

Life shrinks or expands
in proportion to
one's courage.

ANAÏS NIN

It is not the mountain we conquer but ourselves.

SIR EDMUND HILLARY

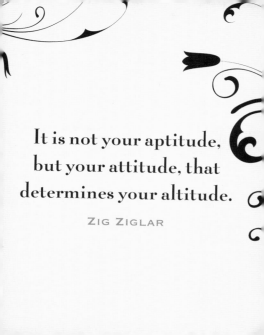

It is not your aptitude,
but your attitude, that
determines your altitude.

ZIG ZIGLAR

I'm a great believer
in luck and I find
the harder I work,
the more I have of it.

THOMAS JEFFERSON

Only those who dare
to fail greatly can ever
achieve greatly.

ROBERT F. KENNEDY

You should always have a big, hairy, audacious goal and believe in that goal and in the fact that you can achieve that goal.

JACK CANFIELD

When there is no enemy
within, the enemies
outside cannot hurt you.

AFRICAN PROVERB

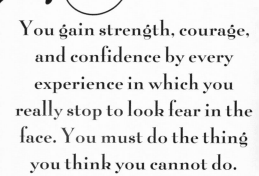

You gain strength, courage, and confidence by every experience in which you really stop to look fear in the face. You must do the thing you think you cannot do.

ELEANOR ROOSEVELT

Edison failed 10,000 times before he made the electric light. Do not be discouraged if you fail a few times.

NAPOLEON HILL

Magic is believing
in yourself. If you can
do that, you can make
anything happen.

JOHANN WOLFGANG VON GOETHE

Take control of your destiny. Believe in yourself. Ignore those who try to discourage you. Avoid negative sources, people, places, things, and habits. Don't give up and don't give in.

WANDA CARTER

Put your future in good hands—your own.

Don't live down to expectations. Go out there and do something remarkable.

WENDY WASSERSTEIN

Whatever you can do, or dream you can do, begin it. Boldness has genius, power, and magic in it. Begin it!

AUTHOR UNKNOWN

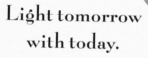

Light tomorrow
with today.

ELIZABETH BARRETT BROWNING

Trust that still, small voice
that says, "This might work
and I'll try it."

DIANE MARIECHILD

If you think you are
too small to be effective,
you have never been in bed
with a mosquito.

BETTY REESE

We do not believe in ourselves
until someone reveals that deep
inside us something is valuable,
worth listening to, worthy of
our trust, sacred to our touch.
Once we believe in ourselves
we can risk curiosity, wonder,
spontaneous delight or any
experience that reveals
the human spirit.

E. E. CUMMINGS

If I have the belief
that I can do it,
I will surely acquire
the capacity to do it,
even if I may not have it
at the beginning.

MAHATMA GANDHI

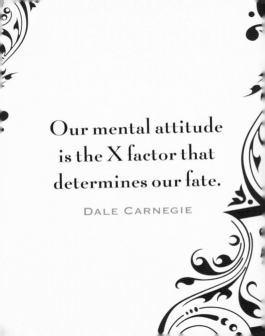

Our mental attitude
is the X factor that
determines our fate.

DALE CARNEGIE

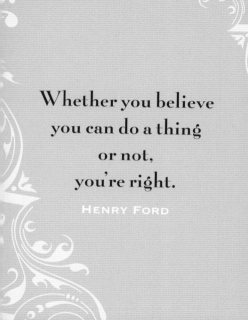

Whether you believe
you can do a thing
or not,
you're right.

HENRY FORD

To be a great champion,
you must believe you are
the best. If you're not,
pretend you are.

MUHAMMAD ALI

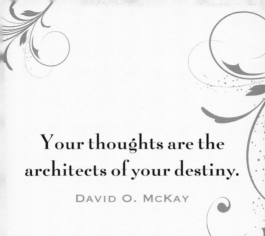

Your thoughts are the architects of your destiny.

DAVID O. MCKAY

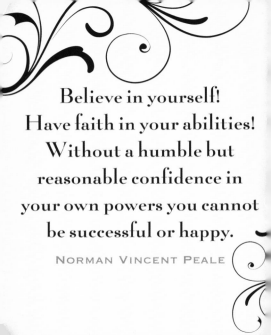

Believe in yourself!
Have faith in your abilities!
Without a humble but
reasonable confidence in
your own powers you cannot
be successful or happy.

NORMAN VINCENT PEALE

The future belongs to those
who believe in the beauty
of their dreams.

ELEANOR ROOSEVELT

As a single footstep will not
make a path on the earth, so a
single thought will not make
a pathway in the mind. To make
a deep physical path, we walk
again and again. To make a deep
mental path, we must think over
and over the kind of thoughts we
wish to dominate our lives.

HENRY DAVID THOREAU

These then are my last words to you. Be not afraid of life. Believe that life is worth living and your belief will help create the fact.

WILLIAM JAMES

Seeing is not believing;
believing is seeing!
You see things, not as
they are, but as you are.

ERIC BUTTERWORTH

Believe that with your
feelings and your work
you are taking part in the
greatest; the more strongly
you cultivate this belief,
the more will reality
and the world go
forth from it.

RAINER MARIA RILKE

If you believe you can,
you probably can. If you
believe you won't, you
most assuredly won't. Belief
is the ignition switch
that gets you off
the launching pad.

DENIS WAITLEY

You can free yourself
from aging by reinterpreting
your body and by grasping
the link between belief
and biology.

DEEPAK CHOPRA

It's so important to believe in yourself. Believe that you can do it, under any circumstances. Because if you believe you can, then you really will.

WALLY "FAMOUS" AMOS

The mind can assert anything and pretend it has proved it. My beliefs I test on my body, on my intuitional consciousness, and when I get a response there, then I accept.

D. H. LAWRENCE

To accomplish great things,
we must not only act, but
also dream; not only plan,
but also believe.

ANATOLE FRANCE

I have learned that
if one advances confidently
in the direction of his dreams,
and endeavors to live the life
he has imagined, he will meet
with a success unexpected
in common hours.

HENRY DAVID THOREAU